THE BUSINESS SUCCESS GUIDE TO CATTLE RANCHING

Comprehensive Insight To Raising, Managing, Profit, Techniques, Best Practices, And Sustainable Strategies For Success

RICHMOND HAMILL

Disclaimer

The information presented in this book is based on the author's personal knowledge and understanding of livestock management. The author is not affiliated with any association, company, business, or individual in the livestock industry. All content is provided for informational purposes only and should not be considered as professional advice. Readers are encouraged to seek professional guidance and conduct their own research before making any decisions based on the information contained in this book. The author and publisher disclaim any liability for any adverse effects or consequences resulting from the use of the information contained herein.

Table of Contents

ABOUT THIS BOOK

This book "Cattle Ranching" serves as an indispensable guide for both novice and experienced ranchers, offering a comprehensive exploration into the multifaceted world of cattle ranching. It begins with an introduction that provides an extensive overview of the practice, tracing its historical roots and evolution while emphasizing its crucial role in agriculture. Readers are acquainted with essential terminology and the myriad benefits those cattle ranching offers, from economic to environmental impacts.

When it comes to selecting the right breed, this book provides a thorough analysis of various cattle breeds. It covers key considerations in breed selection, addressing popular breeds for both beef and dairy production. The discussion extends to the advantages of crossbreeding, presenting strategies to achieve optimal results, thereby empowering ranchers to make informed decisions tailored to their specific goals.

Setting up a ranch is a critical phase, and this book details every essential aspect, from selecting and preparing the land to the necessary infrastructure such as fencing and water sources. It guides readers through effective pasture management and rotation techniques, ensuring sustainable land use. Additionally, it offers practical advice on securing permits and licenses, along with meticulous budgeting and financial planning to ensure a successful and legally compliant operation.

Feeding and nutrition are pivotal to cattle health and productivity. This section elucidates the dietary needs of cattle, various types of feed and forage, and the importance of supplementing their diet with minerals and vitamins. Seasonal feeding strategies and methods to monitor and adjust feed plans are also covered, ensuring that readers can maintain optimal nutrition for their herds year-round.

Cattle health and veterinary care are paramount, and this book addresses common health issues, preventive healthcare measures, and vaccination and deworming schedules. It teaches readers how to recognize signs of illness and the importance of working closely with veterinarians to maintain herd health. This section is designed to equip ranchers with the knowledge to preempt and address health challenges effectively.

Breeding and reproduction are explored in depth, covering the reproductive cycle of cattle, the pros and cons of natural versus artificial insemination, and the management of pregnant cows. It also delves into the calving process and care, offering strategies to improve breeding efficiency, thus maximizing herd productivity and genetic quality.

Handling and transportation are critical for cattle welfare. This book provides safe handling techniques, necessary equipment, and stress reduction methods during handling. It outlines best practices for transporting cattle safely and the legal requirements involved, ensuring that ranchers can move their animals efficiently and humanely.

Marketing and selling cattle are crucial for financial success. This section helps ranchers identify their target market, develop effective pricing strategies, and utilize various marketing channels such as auctions and direct sales. It also covers how to prepare cattle for sale and build lasting relationships with buyers, facilitating successful transactions and business growth.

Record keeping and management are emphasized as vital components of a successful ranch. This book explains the importance of accurate records, the types of records to maintain, and how to use technology for efficient record-keeping. It also covers financial management and budgeting, and how analyzing data can lead to improved decision-making and operational efficiency.

Sustainable ranching practices are explored, highlighting the benefits of adopting environmentally friendly methods. This book discusses soil and water conservation techniques, integrating wildlife and biodiversity, and reducing the carbon footprint. It also looks at future trends in sustainable ranching, providing a forward-thinking perspective for progressive ranchers.

Finally, this book addresses the challenges and risks inherent in cattle ranching. It identifies common challenges and offers risk management strategies, advice on coping with market fluctuations and managing environmental risks like droughts and floods. It emphasizes building resilience in ranching operations, preparing readers to navigate and overcome the adversities they may encounter.

By covering these critical areas in depth, "Cattle Ranching" stands as a comprehensive resource for anyone involved in or aspiring to join the cattle ranching industry, offering practical knowledge and strategies to achieve success in this demanding yet rewarding field.

CHAPTER ONE

Introduction To Cattle Ranching

Overview Of Cattle Ranching

Cattle ranching are the practice of raising herds of cattle on large tracts of land. This agricultural activity is essential for producing meat (beef), milk, and other dairy products, as well as leather and other by-products. Cattle ranching involve several processes, including breeding, raising, and managing cattle, ensuring their health, and optimizing the use of pastureland. For beginners, understanding the basic principles and processes of cattle ranching is crucial to starting a successful and sustainable operation.

To begin cattle ranching, one needs access to adequate land, knowledge of cattle breeds, and a basic understanding of cattle care and management.

It also involves proper fencing, water supply systems, and handling facilities. The initial setup may seem daunting, but with proper planning and management, cattle ranching can be a rewarding venture. Beginners should focus on learning about cattle behavior, nutritional needs, and health management to ensure the well-being of their herd.

History And Evolution

The history of cattle ranching dates back thousands of years. Early humans domesticated cattle for their meat, milk, and hides, which were essential for survival. The practice of cattle ranching has evolved significantly over time. In ancient civilizations, cattle were often herded and grazed on communal lands. With the development of private land ownership, ranching became more structured and organized.

In the Americas, cattle ranching was introduced by Spanish explorers in the 16th century. Ranching practices adapted to the new environments, leading to the development of various cattle breeds suited to different climates and terrains. The introduction of barbed wire in the 19th century revolutionized cattle ranching by allowing ranchers to control grazing areas more effectively. Modern cattle ranching has further evolved with advancements in veterinary medicine, genetics, and technology, enabling ranchers to optimize cattle health and productivity.

Importance In Agriculture

Cattle ranching plays a vital role in the agricultural economy. It is a major source of meat and dairy products, which are essential components of the human diet. Cattle ranching also contributes to the leather industry, providing raw materials for various goods such as clothing, footwear, and accessories. Moreover, cattle ranching supports rural economies by providing employment opportunities and supporting related industries such as feed production, transportation, and veterinary services.

Sustainable cattle ranching practices also contribute to environmental conservation. Properly managed grazing can promote healthy grasslands, reduce soil erosion, and enhance biodiversity. Additionally, cattle can convert inedible plant materials into high-quality protein, making them an efficient means of food production. As the global population continues to grow, the importance of sustainable and efficient cattle ranching practices will only increase.

Basic Terminology

Understanding the basic terminology used in cattle ranching is essential for beginners. Here are some key terms:

Herd: A group of cattle.

Bull: A mature male cattle used for breeding.

Cow: A mature female cattle that has given birth.

Heifer: A young female cattle that has not yet given birth.

Steer A castrated male cattle raised for meat.

Calf: A young cattle, usually under one year old.

Breeding: The process of mating cattle to produce offspring.

Grazing: Allowing cattle to feed on pastureland.

Feedlot: A confined area where cattle are fed a high-energy diet to promote rapid growth.

Weaning: The process of separating calves from their mothers to begin independent feeding.

Key Benefits Of Cattle Ranching

Cattle ranching offer numerous benefits, both economic and environmental. Economically, it provides a steady income stream for ranchers through the sale of meat, dairy products, and by-products. It also supports rural communities by creating jobs and promoting local businesses. Environmentally, well-managed cattle ranching can contribute to land conservation, promote healthy ecosystems, and improve soil health through proper grazing practices.

Additionally, cattle ranching can enhance food security by providing a reliable source of high-quality protein. It also offers opportunities for diversification, as ranchers can raise different breeds for various purposes, such as meat production, dairy farming, or breeding stock.

CHAPTER TWO

Choosing The Right Breed

Overview Of Cattle Breeds

Selecting the right breed of cattle is crucial for the success of your ranching operation. Each breed has its unique characteristics, including physical traits, temperament, and suitability for specific environmental conditions. The two main categories of cattle are beef and dairy cattle, each bred for distinct purposes.

Beef cattle are primarily raised for meat production. They are generally stockier and more muscular compared to dairy cattle. Some common beef cattle breeds include Angus, Hereford, and Charolais. Dairy cattle, on the other hand, are bred for milk production.

These breeds, such as Holstein, Jersey, and Guernsey, are typically leaner and have higher milk yields.

When choosing a breed, it is essential to consider factors such as climate adaptability, feed efficiency, growth rate, and overall hardiness. Additionally, understanding the market demand and your personal preferences can help in making an informed decision.

Factors To Consider In Breed Selection

Climate Adaptability

One of the most important factors in selecting a cattle breed is its adaptability to your local climate. Some breeds are better suited for hot, arid climates, while others thrive in cooler, wetter environments. For instance, Brahman cattle are known for their heat tolerance and are often used in tropical and subtropical regions. In contrast, Angus cattle perform well in cooler climates.

Feed Efficiency

Feed efficiency refers to the amount of feed required to produce a certain amount of weight gain or milk. Some breeds convert feed into body mass or milk more efficiently than others. For beef production, breeds like Angus and Hereford are known for their efficient feed conversion, which can lead to lower feeding costs and higher profitability. In dairy cattle, Holsteins are renowned for their high milk yield per unit of feed.

Growth Rate and Maturity

Different breeds have varying growth rates and ages at which they reach maturity. Breeds with faster growth rates can be more profitable in beef production, as they reach market weight more quickly. Charolais cattle, for example, are known for their rapid growth and large frame. For dairy cattle, it is essential to consider the age at which heifers start producing milk, as earlier maturity can lead to quicker returns on investment.

Popular Breeds For Beef Production

Angus

Angus cattle are one of the most popular beef breeds in the world, known for their excellent meat quality and marbling. They are hardy animals that adapt well to various climates and are relatively easy to manage. Angus cattle are also known for their high fertility rates and good maternal instincts, making them a preferred choice for many ranchers.

Hereford

Hereford cattle are another widely recognized beef breed, appreciated for their docile temperament and robust health. They are highly adaptable to different environmental conditions and have strong disease resistance. Herefords are known for their efficient feed conversion and excellent meat quality, making them a reliable choice for beef production.

Charolais

Charolais cattle are renowned for their rapid growth rate and large body size. They are typically white or cream-colored and are known for producing lean, high-quality beef. Charolais are often used in crossbreeding programs to improve the growth rate and meat quality of other breeds. Their ability to thrive in various climates and their strong muscling make them a valuable breed for beef ranchers.

Popular Breeds For Dairy Production

Holstein

Holstein cattle are the most common dairy breed globally, recognized for their distinctive black-and-white markings and exceptional milk production. They have the highest milk yield among dairy breeds, making them the backbone of the dairy industry. Holsteins are known for their efficiency in converting feed into milk and their adaptability to different management systems.

Jersey

Jersey cattle are smaller than Holsteins but are highly valued for their rich, high-fat-content milk. This breed is known for its docile temperament, ease of calving, and efficient feed conversion. Jerseys are adaptable to various climates and are often preferred by dairy farmers who prioritize milk quality over quantity.

Guernsey

Guernsey cattle are famous for their golden-yellow milk, which is high in beta-carotene and butterfat. They are medium-sized cows with a gentle disposition and excellent feed efficiency. Guernseys are well-suited to grass-based dairy systems and are known for their high fertility rates and ease of management.

Crossbreeding For Optimal Results

Crossbreeding involves mating cattle of different breeds to combine desirable traits from both parents. This practice can lead to hybrid vigor, or heterosis, which often results in offspring that are healthier, more fertile, and more productive than their purebred counterparts.

Benefits of Crossbreeding

Crossbreeding can improve various traits such as growth rate, feed efficiency, disease resistance, and overall hardiness. For beef production, crossbreeding can enhance meat quality and yield, while in dairy production, it can boost milk production and improve cow health. For example, crossing Angus with Hereford can produce calves that grow quickly and have excellent meat quality, while crossing Holstein with Jersey can result in cows with high milk yield and superior milk fat content.

Implementing Crossbreeding Programs

To implement a successful crossbreeding program, it is essential to select breeds that complement each other and align with your production goals. Begin by evaluating the strengths and weaknesses of your existing herd and identifying areas for improvement. Choose breeds that can enhance these traits and plan the mating schedule accordingly.

Maintain detailed records of breeding, calving, and performance data to track the success of your crossbreeding program. Over time, you can refine your breeding strategy to optimize the performance and productivity of your herd.

By understanding the characteristics of different cattle breeds and implementing strategic crossbreeding programs, you can enhance the productivity and profitability of your cattle ranching operation.

CHAPTER THREE

Setting Up Your Ranch

Land Selection And Preparation

Selecting the right land is the foundation of a successful cattle ranch. The first step is to identify a location with ample space, as cattle need plenty of room to graze. Ideally, the land should be flat or gently rolling to prevent soil erosion and make it easier to manage. You should also ensure the land has fertile soil to support robust pasture growth.

Once you have identified a potential location, conduct a soil test to determine its suitability for growing pasture. This involves collecting soil samples from various parts of the land and sending them to a laboratory for analysis. The results will guide you in amending the soil with the necessary nutrients. After amending the soil, you can begin to prepare the land by removing any debris, large rocks, or unwanted vegetation that could hinder pasture growth or harm the cattle.

The final step in land preparation is to establish a suitable pasture. This can be done by planting a mix of grasses and legumes that are appropriate for your climate and soil type. It's important to choose species that are resilient, nutritious, and able to thrive throughout the seasons. Regularly monitor the pasture to ensure it remains healthy and can sustain your cattle's nutritional needs.

Necessary Infrastructure (Fencing, Water Sources)

Once your land is prepared, it's time to set up the necessary infrastructure. Fencing is crucial for keeping your cattle contained and safe from predators.

There are various types of fencing to consider, including barbed wire, electric fencing, and high-tensile wire. Choose a fencing type that suits your budget and is effective for the size and breed of cattle you plan to raise. Ensure the fence is sturdy and regularly check for any damages that need repair.

Water is another essential resource for cattle, as they need a constant supply of clean water for drinking and cooling off. Depending on the size of your ranch, you can either install troughs connected to a reliable water source or create ponds. Ponds should be designed to capture and store rainwater, providing a sustainable water supply. Installing automatic waterers in each paddock can help ensure that your cattle always have access to fresh water.

Additionally, consider setting up shelters to protect your cattle from extreme weather conditions. Simple structures such as open-sided sheds or windbreaks can provide shade in the summer and protection from cold winds in the winter. These shelters should be strategically placed in areas where cattle tend to congregate.

Pasture Management And Rotation

Effective pasture management and rotation are key to maintaining the health of your land and cattle. Rotational grazing involves dividing your pasture into several smaller paddocks and moving your cattle from one paddock to another regularly. This allows each paddock time to rest and recover, promoting regrowth and reducing the risk of overgrazing.

Begin by designing a rotational grazing plan. This plan should consider the number of paddocks, the size of your herd, and the growth rate of your pasture. A common approach is to use a four-paddock system, where cattle are moved every few days to a new paddock.

Monitor the pasture's growth and adjust the rotation schedule as needed to ensure optimal regrowth and forage quality.

In addition to rotational grazing, regular pasture maintenance is necessary. This includes reseeding bare areas, controlling weeds, and fertilizing the soil as needed. Regular soil testing can help determine the specific nutrients required to maintain healthy pasture growth. By following these practices, you can ensure a sustainable and productive pasture for your cattle.

Securing Permits And Licenses

Before fully establishing your cattle ranch, it is essential to secure the necessary permits and licenses. These legal requirements vary depending on your location and the scale of your operation. Typically, you will need a business license, a livestock operation permit, and possibly environmental permits if your ranching activities impact local water sources or wildlife habitats.

Start by contacting your local agricultural extension office or department of agriculture to determine the specific permits and licenses required in your area. They can provide you with the necessary application forms and guide you through the process. Ensure you have all the required documentation, such as land ownership or lease agreements, environmental impact assessments, and business plans.

It's also important to familiarize yourself with any zoning regulations that may affect your ranch. Some areas have restrictions on livestock density, waste management, and the use of certain chemicals. Adhering to these regulations not only keeps you compliant with the law but also helps protect the environment and community around your ranch.

Budgeting And Financial Planning

Financial planning is a critical aspect of setting up your ranch. Start by creating a detailed budget that outlines all the costs involved in establishing and running your operation. This should include expenses for land acquisition or lease, fencing, water systems, pasture establishment, livestock purchase, feed, veterinary care, labor, and any other operational costs.

To accurately estimate these costs, conduct thorough research or consult with experienced ranchers. Consider both initial setup costs and ongoing operational expenses. It's also wise to build a financial cushion to cover unexpected costs, such as emergency veterinary care or equipment repairs.

Once you have a comprehensive budget, explore different financing options. These may include personal savings, bank loans, agricultural grants, or partnerships with other investors. Present a solid business plan to potential lenders or investors to increase your chances of securing funding. Your business plan should include detailed financial projections, demonstrating how your ranch will generate revenue and achieve profitability.

Regularly review and update your financial plan to reflect changes in your operation or market conditions. Keeping a close eye on your finances ensures you can make informed decisions and maintain the financial health of your ranch.

CHAPTER FOUR

Feeding And Nutrition

Understanding Cattle Dietary Needs

Cattle dietary needs are primarily determined by their age, weight, production stage, and overall health. Understanding these needs is essential for ensuring that cattle are healthy, productive, and well-nourished. For instance, growing calves require a diet high in protein to support their rapid growth, while lactating cows need additional energy to produce milk. Beef cattle, on the other hand, require a balanced diet to maintain weight and muscle mass for market readiness.

To meet these varying needs, cattle diets are typically composed of roughages, concentrates, minerals, and vitamins. Roughages include grasses and hay, which are high in fiber but low in energy. Concentrates, such as grains and by-products, provide the necessary energy and protein. It is crucial to provide a balanced mix of these components to avoid deficiencies or excesses that could lead to health issues.

Farmers should regularly assess their cattle's body condition and adjust feeding plans accordingly. Body condition scoring (BCS) is a practical method used to evaluate the health and nutritional status of cattle by assessing fat cover and muscle mass. Scores range from 1 (emaciated) to 9 (obese), with a score of 5-6 being ideal for most cattle. Regular monitoring and adjustments help maintain optimal health and productivity.

Types Of Feed And Forage

Cattle feed and forage can be broadly categorized into roughages and concentrates. Roughages include pasture grasses, hay, silage, and crop residues, all of which are essential for providing the fiber necessary for proper rumen function. Common pasture grasses include Bermuda grass, Timothy grass, and Orchard grass. Hay can be made from various grasses or legumes, such as alfalfa, which is particularly nutritious.

Silage, made from fermented crops like corn or sorghum, is a popular feed during the winter months when pasture is scarce. It is high in energy and provides a good source of nutrients when fresh forage is not available. Crop residues, such as corn stalks and wheat straw, can also be used as roughages, although they are typically lower in nutritional value.

Concentrates include grains (corn, barley, oats), protein supplements (soybean meal, cottonseed meal), and by-products (beet pulp, brewers grains). These feeds are energy-dense and help meet the higher nutritional demands of growing, lactating, or finishing cattle. It is important to balance the use of concentrates with roughage to ensure a well-rounded diet that supports health and productivity.

Supplementing Diet With Minerals And Vitamins

Minerals and vitamins are critical components of cattle nutrition, necessary for various bodily functions, including bone development, immune response, and reproductive performance. Common mineral supplements include salt, calcium, phosphorus, and trace minerals such as zinc, copper, and selenium.

These can be provided through mineral blocks, loose minerals, or mixed into the feed.

Vitamins such as A, D, and E are also essential. Vitamin A is crucial for vision and immune function, while vitamin D supports bone health, and vitamin E acts as an antioxidant. These vitamins can be provided through fortified feeds or supplements, particularly when cattle do not have access to fresh pasture, which is a natural source of many vitamins.

To ensure cattle receive adequate minerals and vitamins, farmers should provide free-choice mineral feeders in pastures and regularly monitor intake. Consulting with a veterinarian or an animal nutritionist can help design a supplementation program tailored to the specific needs of the herd, considering factors like soil mineral content and forage quality.

Seasonal Feeding Strategies

Seasonal changes significantly impact cattle feeding strategies. During spring and summer, when pasture forage is abundant, cattle can graze freely, which reduces the need for supplemental feed. However, it is important to manage grazing to prevent overgrazing and ensure pasture regrowth. Rotational grazing systems, where cattle are moved between pastures, can help maintain forage availability and quality.

In the fall, as pasture growth slows, supplemental feeding may be necessary to maintain nutritional levels. Hay and silage are commonly used during this period. Ensuring that cattle have access to high-quality forage and monitoring body conditions will help prepare them for the winter months.

Winter feeding requires careful planning, as fresh forage is limited. Stored feeds such as hay and silage become primary sources of nutrition. Providing a balanced diet with adequate energy, protein, and fiber is crucial to maintain body condition and health. Additionally, providing windbreaks and shelter can help reduce the energy requirements of cattle in cold weather.

Monitoring And Adjusting Feed Plans

Regular monitoring and adjusting feed plans are vital to maintaining cattle health and productivity. This involves observing cattle behavior, assessing body condition scores, and monitoring feed intake and weight gain. By keeping detailed records of feed types, amounts, and cattle performance, farmers can identify trends and make informed adjustments to the feeding plan.

Implementing a feed testing program can provide valuable insights into the nutritional content of forages and supplements. Testing can reveal deficiencies or imbalances that need to be addressed to optimize cattle nutrition. Working with a nutritionist can help interpret test results and develop a tailored feeding strategy.

Incorporating technology, such as automated feeders and mobile apps for record-keeping, can streamline the process of monitoring and adjusting feed plans. These tools can provide real-time data and make it easier to track and manage cattle nutrition, ensuring that the herd remains healthy and productive year-round.

CHAPTER FIVE

Cattle Health And Veterinary Care

Common Health Issues In Cattle

Cattle are prone to several common health issues that every rancher should be aware of. Understanding these ailments can help in early detection and treatment, ensuring the well-being of the herd.

1.   Bovine Respiratory Disease (BRD): This is a complex of bacterial and viral infections that affect the respiratory tract of cattle. Symptoms include coughing, nasal discharge, and difficulty breathing. To prevent BRD, ensure proper ventilation in housing areas and reduce stress factors such as overcrowding.

2.   **Mastitis:** This is an infection of the udder tissue, commonly caused by bacteria entering the teat. Symptoms include swelling, heat, and pain in the udder, along with abnormal milk secretion. Maintaining good hygiene during milking and proper nutrition can help prevent mastitis.

3.   **Foot Rot:** This bacterial infection affects the hooves, leading to lameness and swelling. It often occurs in wet, muddy conditions. Regular hoof trimming and maintaining dry, clean living conditions can help prevent foot rot.

4.   **Bloat:** Bloat occurs when gas accumulates in the rumen, causing the animal's abdomen to swell. It can be life-threatening if not treated promptly. Prevent bloat by managing your diet carefully, avoiding sudden changes in feed, and providing access to fresh water.

Preventive Healthcare Measures

Preventive healthcare is crucial in maintaining a healthy cattle herd. By implementing the following measures, you can reduce the incidence of diseases and improve overall herd health.

1. **Hygiene and Sanitation:** Keep living areas clean and dry to prevent the spread of pathogens. Regularly clean feeding and watering equipment to reduce contamination.

2. **Nutrition:** Provide a balanced diet that meets the nutritional needs of your cattle. Ensure they have access to clean water and high-quality feed. Supplement their diet with the necessary minerals and vitamins.

3. **Biosecurity:** Implement biosecurity measures to prevent the introduction of new diseases. Quarantine new animals before introducing them to

the herd, and limit access to your farm to essential personnel only.

4.   **Regular Health Checks:** Conduct regular health checks to monitor the condition of your cattle. Look for signs of illness, injury, or abnormalities. Early detection is key to effective treatment.

Vaccination And Deworming Schedules

Vaccination and deworming are essential components of a cattle health management plan. They help protect your herd from infectious diseases and parasitic infestations.

1.   Vaccination Schedule:

Calves: Begin vaccinating calves at 3-4 months of age with vaccines for diseases such as Bovine Respiratory Syncytial Virus (BRSV), Infectious

Bovine Rhinotracheitis (IBR), and Bovine Viral Diarrhea (BVD).

Yearlings: Administer booster vaccines to yearlings to ensure continued protection.

Adult Cattle: Maintain an annual vaccination schedule for adult cattle, including vaccines for leptospirosis, clostridial diseases, and other region-specific diseases.

2. Deworming Schedule:

Calves: Deworm calves at 6-8 weeks of age and repeat every 6-8 weeks until they are weaned.

Yearlings: Deworm yearlings 2-3 times per year, depending on pasture conditions and parasite load.

Adult Cattle: Deworm adult cattle at least twice a year, ideally before grazing season and after the first frost to minimize parasite burden.

Recognizing Signs Of Illness

Early detection of illness is crucial in managing cattle health. Recognize the following signs of illness and take prompt action:

1.   Behavioral Changes: Look for changes in behavior, such as lethargy, decreased appetite, or isolation from the herd. These can be early indicators of illness.

2.   Physical Symptoms: Monitor for physical symptoms such as coughing, nasal discharge, diarrhea, or lameness. Any sudden changes in physical appearance, like swelling or abnormal secretions, should be addressed immediately.

3.   Vital Signs: Regularly check vital signs, including temperature, heart rate, and respiratory rate. Fever, increased heart rate, or labored breathing can indicate an underlying health issue.

4.	**Milk Production:** In lactating cows, a sudden drop in milk production can be a sign of illness. Pay attention to udder health and milk quality.

Working With A Veterinarian

Collaborating with a veterinarian is essential for maintaining the health of your cattle. Here's how to build an effective working relationship with your vet:

1.	**Routine Check-ups:** Schedule regular veterinary check-ups to assess the health of your herd. These check-ups can help in early detection of potential health issues.

2.	**Emergency Care:** Establish a protocol for emergency veterinary care. Ensure you have the veterinarian's contact information readily available and know the signs that warrant immediate veterinary attention.

3.   Health Records: Keep detailed health records for each animal. Document vaccinations, deworming, treatments, and any health issues. This information helps the veterinarian make informed decisions and track the health history of your herd.

4.   Education and Training: Work with your veterinarian to educate yourself and your staff on cattle health management. Attend workshops and training sessions to stay updated on the latest best practices in cattle healthcare.

By understanding common health issues, implementing preventive measures, adhering to vaccination and deworming schedules, recognizing signs of illness, and working closely with a veterinarian, you can ensure the well-being of your cattle herd and improve overall productivity.

CHAPTER SIX

Breeding And Reproduction

Understanding The Cattle Reproductive Cycle

The reproductive cycle of cattle is a crucial aspect of successful cattle ranching. Understanding this cycle helps ranchers plan for breeding, manage pregnancies, and ensure the health of both cows and calves. The estrous cycle, or heat cycle, in cows, typically lasts 21 days, but it can range from 18 to 24 days. This cycle is divided into several stages: proestrus, estrus, metestrus, and diestrus.

During proestrus, which lasts about 3 days, the cow's body prepares for ovulation. The hormone estrogen rises, leading to physical and behavioral changes. Estrus, or heat, follows and lasts for 12 to 24 hours. This is when the cow is most fertile and receptive to mating. Signs of estrus include restlessness, increased vocalization, and standing to be mounted by other cows.

Metestrus, lasting about 3 to 4 days, occurs after ovulation. During this phase, the hormone progesterone increases, preparing the uterus for a potential pregnancy. If the cow does not conceive, the cycle moves into diestrus, which lasts about 14 to 18 days. Progesterone remains high to support pregnancy if conception occurs, or it will decline to start a new cycle if the cow is not pregnant.

Monitoring the estrous cycle is essential for effective breeding management. Using visual observation, heat detection aids, or hormone testing can help identify the optimal breeding time. Understanding these stages allows ranchers to plan and manage their herds more efficiently.

Natural Vs. Artificial Insemination

Breeding cattle can be done through natural mating or artificial insemination (AI). Each method has its benefits and challenges, and choosing the right approach depends on the rancher's goals, resources, and management style.

Natural mating involves a bull breeding with cows directly. This method is straightforward and often preferred by smaller operations due to its simplicity and lower initial costs. Bulls are usually kept with the herd or introduced to cows during their estrus period. It's essential to select bulls with desirable traits and good health to ensure the quality of the offspring.

Artificial insemination, on the other hand, allows for more controlled breeding and access to superior genetics. AI involves collecting semen from a selected bull and manually depositing it into the cow's reproductive tract during estrus. This method requires more skill and knowledge but offers significant advantages. AI enables ranchers to use semen from top-quality bulls worldwide, improve genetic diversity, and reduce the risk of disease transmission.

To perform AI, ranchers need proper training and equipment, such as AI guns and semen storage facilities. Timing is critical, as insemination should occur within 12 hours of detecting estrus. Hormone synchronization protocols can also be used to manage breeding schedules more effectively.

Both natural mating and AI have their place in cattle ranching. Combining both methods can optimize breeding programs, improve herd genetics, and enhance overall productivity.

Managing Pregnant Cows

Proper management of pregnant cows is vital to ensure the health of both the mother and the developing calf. During pregnancy, cows require special care and attention to maintain their well-being and support fetal development. Key aspects of managing pregnant cows include nutrition, health monitoring, and stress reduction.

Nutrition plays a crucial role in the health of pregnant cows. Providing a balanced diet with adequate energy, protein, vitamins, and minerals is essential. Pregnant cows have higher nutritional needs, especially in the last trimester when fetal growth is most rapid. Ensure access to high-quality forage, supplements, and clean water. Monitoring body condition scores helps assess nutritional status and make necessary adjustments.

Health monitoring involves regular veterinary check-ups, vaccinations, and parasite control. Pregnant cows should be vaccinated against diseases that could affect pregnancy or calf health. Monitoring for signs of illness or complications, such as lameness or udder issues, is crucial. Implementing biosecurity measures helps prevent disease outbreaks.

Reducing stress is also important for pregnant cows. Stress can negatively impact pregnancy and calf development. Provide a calm and comfortable environment, minimize handling, and avoid overcrowding. Ensure cows have adequate shelter and protection from extreme weather conditions.

Creating a calving plan is essential for managing pregnant cows. This plan should include monitoring expected calving dates, preparing calving facilities, and having necessary supplies on hand. Regularly observing cows as they approach their due dates helps detect early signs of labor and address any complications promptly.

Calving Process And Care

The calving process is a critical period that requires careful observation and timely intervention to ensure the health of both the cow and the calf. Understanding the stages of calving and providing appropriate care can significantly improve outcomes.

Calving is divided into three stages: early labor, active labor, and delivery. Early labor, or the preparatory stage, can last up to 24 hours. During this stage, the cow becomes restless, isolates herself, and shows signs of discomfort. The cervix begins to dilate, and uterine contractions start. Monitoring the cow closely during this stage is important, but intervention is usually not necessary.

Active labor follows and typically lasts 2 to 6 hours. This stage involves stronger contractions and the cow lying down and getting up frequently. The amniotic sac becomes visible, and the calf starts moving into the birth canal. If the cow is not making progress after an hour of active labor, assistance may be needed.

The delivery stage is when the calf is born. Ideally, this should happen quickly once the cow starts pushing. If the calf is not delivered within 2 hours of the onset of active labor, assistance may be required. When assisting, ensure proper hygiene and be gentle to avoid injuring the cow or the calf. If complications arise, such as a breech position or large calf, contact a veterinarian immediately.

After delivery, ensure the calf is breathing and clear any mucus from its nose and mouth. Allow the cow to lick the calf, which stimulates breathing and bonding.

Provide the calf with colostrum within the first few hours, as it is crucial for immunity. Monitor the cow for signs of retained placenta or other post-calving issues.

Providing a clean, dry, and safe environment for both the cow and the calf is essential. Ensure the calf is warm, especially in cold weather, and monitor its health closely in the first few days.

Improving Breeding Efficiency

Improving breeding efficiency is vital for maximizing productivity and profitability in cattle ranching. Several strategies can enhance breeding success and optimize herd performance.

Firstly, implementing a comprehensive health management program is crucial. Regular veterinary check-ups, vaccinations, and parasite control ensure cows are in optimal health for breeding.

Monitoring body condition scores helps maintain cows at an ideal weight, as both underweight and overweight cows can experience reproductive issues.

Using reproductive technologies such as estrus synchronization and artificial insemination (AI) can significantly improve breeding efficiency. Estrus synchronization involves administering hormones to synchronize the estrous cycles of cows, allowing for controlled breeding schedules. This practice helps ensure a higher percentage of cows are bred within a specific timeframe, reducing the calving interval.

AI offers access to superior genetics and allows for more precise breeding. Selecting high-quality semen from bulls with desirable traits can improve the genetic quality of the herd. Combining AI with estrus synchronization can enhance the success rate of insemination.

Record-keeping is essential for improving breeding efficiency. Keeping detailed records of breeding dates, estrus cycles, pregnancy checks, and calving outcomes helps identify patterns and make informed management decisions. Analyzing these records can highlight areas for improvement and optimize breeding programs.

Nutrition plays a critical role in breeding efficiency. Providing a balanced diet with adequate energy, protein, and minerals supports reproductive health. Special attention should be given to the nutritional needs of cows during breeding, pregnancy, and lactation. Ensuring cows are in good body condition improves their chances of successful conception and healthy pregnancies.

Finally, selecting fertility traits when breeding replacements can enhance breeding efficiency. Choosing heifers and bulls with proven fertility and reproductive longevity can lead to more consistent breeding success in the herd.

CHAPTER SEVEN

Handling And Transportation

Safe Cattle Handling Techniques

Handling cattle safely and effectively is crucial for the well-being of both the animals and the handlers. Understanding the basic principles and techniques for safe cattle handling ensures that the process is smooth and minimizes stress for the cattle.

Basic Principles Of Safe Handling

Safe cattle handling begins with a clear understanding of the animal's behavior and body language. Cattle are prey animals, which means they are naturally inclined to be cautious and sometimes fearful. Approach them calmly and quietly, avoiding sudden movements or loud noises that could startle them.

Use a low, soothing voice when speaking to them. Always handle cattle in a manner that respects their space and comfort levels.

Techniques For Handling

1.   Use **Proper Body Positioning:** When working with cattle, positioning yourself correctly is key. Stand beside the animal, not directly in front or behind it, to avoid startling it. If you need to move the animal, position yourself so that you are directing its movement rather than forcing it. Cattle respond better to gentle guidance.

2.   **Employ the Use of Cattle Prods and Sticks:** While handling tools like cattle prods or sticks can be useful, they should be used sparingly and as a last resort. The goal is to move cattle using as little force as possible. Use prods and sticks to gently guide the cattle in the desired direction rather than as instruments of coercion.

3.   Train for Safety: Regular handling and training sessions help cattle become accustomed to human interaction. This familiarity can reduce their stress levels and make future handling easier. Consistency and positive reinforcement during these sessions help build trust between the cattle and handlers.

Equipment For Handling Cattle

Selecting the right equipment for handling cattle is essential for both efficiency and safety. The equipment used can significantly impact the ease with which cattle are managed and their overall stress levels.

Essential Equipment

1.   Cattle Chutes and Headgates: Cattle chutes are designed to hold cattle securely while they are being examined or treated. The chute should be sturdy and adjustable to accommodate different sizes

of cattle. Headgates are used to immobilize the animal's head, making it easier to perform tasks like vaccinations or branding.

2.   Sorting Panels and Alleys: Sorting panels are used to guide cattle into specific areas, such as pens or chutes. They should be designed to be flexible and easy to move, allowing for efficient sorting and movement of cattle. Alleys are narrow pathways that lead cattle to different areas, and they should be wide enough to allow comfortable movement without causing stress.

3.   Cattle Prods and Lead Ropes: Cattle prods should be used with caution and only when necessary. Lead ropes help in guiding cattle from one place to another and can be used to encourage movement in a controlled manner.

Maintenance And Safety

Regular maintenance of handling equipment is crucial to ensure its effectiveness and safety. Check equipment for wear and tear and repair or replace any damaged parts promptly. Ensure that all equipment is clean and free from sharp edges or other hazards that could injure the cattle.

Stress Reduction During Handling

Minimizing stress during cattle handling is important for maintaining the health and productivity of the animals. Stress can lead to a range of issues, including reduced growth rates and increased susceptibility to illness.

Techniques For Stress Reduction

1. **Familiarize Cattle with Their Environment:** Cattle that are accustomed to their environment are less likely to become stressed during handling. Ensure that the handling areas are well-lit, clean, and free from any sudden changes or distractions. Familiarity with the surroundings can make cattle feel more secure.

2. **Implement a Calm Approach:** Approach cattle calmly and at a steady pace. Avoid loud noises and sudden movements, which can startle and stress the animals. Use gentle, consistent handling techniques to help the cattle remain calm.

3. **Provide Adequate Space:** Allow enough space for cattle to move comfortably. Overcrowding can lead to increased stress and aggression among the animals. Ensure that handling areas are designed to

prevent crowding and provide sufficient room for the cattle to move freely.

Monitoring Stress Levels

Regularly observe the cattle for signs of stress, such as excessive vocalization, pacing, or aggression. Adjust handling practices as needed to reduce stress and improve the overall well-being of the animals.

Transporting Cattle Safely

Transporting cattle involves several key considerations to ensure their safety and comfort throughout the journey. Proper planning and execution of transportation procedures are essential to minimize stress and potential health issues.

Preparation For Transportation

1.　　Check Transportation Vehicles: Ensure that the vehicle is well-maintained and designed for cattle. The vehicle should be clean, with adequate ventilation and non-slip flooring. Inspect the vehicle for any hazards that could injure the cattle during transit.

2.　　Plan the Journey: Plan the transportation route to minimize travel time and avoid rough or dangerous roads. Ensure that there are appropriate facilities for feeding and watering the cattle if the journey is long.

3.　　Loading and Unloading: Load cattle calmly and efficiently to prevent stress and injury. Use sorting panels and guides to direct the cattle into the vehicle without forcing them. When unloading, ensure that the area is safe and secure to prevent accidents.

During Transportation

1. **Monitor Conditions:** Regularly check the conditions within the transport vehicle, including ventilation and temperature. Ensure that the cattle have access to water if the journey is extended.

2. **Handle Emergencies:** Be prepared to handle any emergencies that may arise during transportation, such as illness or injury. Have a first aid kit and contact information for a veterinarian readily available.

Legal Requirements For Transportation

Transporting cattle involves adhering to various legal requirements to ensure compliance with regulations and promote animal welfare.

Understanding Regulations

1.   **Licensing and Certification:** Ensure that you have the necessary licenses and certifications required for transporting cattle. This may include specific permits for livestock transport and compliance with local or national regulations.

2.   **Health and Safety Standards:** Adhere to health and safety standards related to the transport of cattle. This includes ensuring that the transport vehicle meets regulatory requirements for ventilation, sanitation, and animal welfare.

3.   **Documentation:** Maintain accurate records of the cattle being transported, including health certificates, proof of ownership, and transportation permits. These documents may be required for inspection by regulatory authorities.

Compliance And Monitoring

1. **Regular Inspections:** Conduct regular inspections of your transportation practices to ensure compliance with legal requirements. Stay informed about any changes in regulations that may affect your transportation practices.

2. **Training and Education:** Provide training for all individuals involved in cattle transportation to ensure they understand and comply with legal requirements and best practices for animal welfare.

CHAPTER EIGHT

Marketing And Selling Your Cattle

Identifying Your Target Market

Identifying your target market is a crucial first step in marketing and selling your cattle. Start by understanding the different types of buyers who are interested in purchasing cattle. This may include local farmers, feedlots, meat processors, and even exporters. Each of these buyer types has distinct needs and preferences. Local farmers might be interested in breeding stock or feeder cattle, while meat processors may look for cattle with specific weight and quality characteristics.

To identify your target market, conduct market research within your local area and beyond. Attend agricultural fairs, cattle shows, and livestock auctions to network and gather insights about potential buyers. Use surveys or interviews with existing customers to understand their preferences. Online resources and industry reports can also provide valuable data. Additionally, consider the demand for different types of cattle, such as organic or grass-fed, which may appeal to niche markets.

Once you have gathered this information, segment your market based on criteria such as location, cattle type, and buyer preferences. Tailor your marketing efforts to address the specific needs and interests of each segment. This targeted approach helps in crafting effective marketing messages and strategies that resonate with your potential buyers.

Pricing Strategies

Setting the right price for your cattle involves balancing profitability with market competitiveness. Begin by researching current market prices for cattle in your area and beyond.

Utilize resources like local livestock auctions, agricultural extension services, and industry reports to get an understanding of prevailing prices. Consider factors such as the age, breed, weight, and health of your cattle when determining the price.

One effective pricing strategy is to use a cost-plus approach. Calculate your total costs, including feed, veterinary care, and any other expenses associated with raising your cattle. Add a reasonable profit margin to these costs to set your selling price. Ensure that your price covers all your costs and provides a profit while remaining competitive with market rates.

Another approach is value-based pricing, where you set your price based on the perceived value of your cattle to buyers. For instance, if your cattle are of a premium breed or have superior genetics, you might be able to command a higher price. Regularly review and adjust your pricing strategy based on market fluctuations and changes in buyer demand to stay competitive and maximize profitability.

Marketing Channels (Auctions, Direct Sales)

Choosing the right marketing channel for selling your cattle is essential for reaching potential buyers and achieving a successful sale. Auctions are a popular and effective channel, allowing you to sell cattle quickly and often at competitive prices. Participate in local livestock auctions or regional events to expose your cattle to a wide audience. Ensure that you understand the auction process, including registration, fees, and the auctioneer's terms.

Direct sales are another valuable marketing channel. This involves selling your cattle directly to buyers without intermediaries.

Build relationships with local farmers, feedlots, and meat processors who may be interested in purchasing cattle. Establish a strong online presence through a website or social media platforms to attract potential buyers. You can also use direct marketing techniques such as email campaigns or advertisements in agricultural publications to reach your target audience.

Evaluate the benefits of each channel based on your specific needs and goals. Auctions may provide a quick sale and access to a broad market, while direct sales offer the opportunity to build long-term relationships with buyers and potentially achieve higher prices. Utilize a combination of channels to maximize your reach and increase the likelihood of successful sales.

Preparing Cattle For Sale

Preparing your cattle for sale is crucial for achieving the best possible price and ensuring a smooth transaction. Start by ensuring that your cattle are in optimal health. Regular veterinary care, including vaccinations and deworming, is essential to maintaining their health and preventing diseases. Ensure that your cattle are well-fed and in good condition, as this will positively impact their weight and appearance.

Grooming and handling are also important aspects of preparation. Clean and trim the cattle's hooves, and ensure that their coats are free of dirt and debris. Spend time working with your cattle to familiarize them with handling and reduce stress during the sale process. A well-groomed and calm animal is more likely to attract positive attention from buyers.

Before the sale, gather and organize any necessary documentation, such as health records, breeding certificates, and ownership papers. This information reassures buyers about the quality and history of the cattle. Ensure that you have clear and accurate records to provide to potential buyers, enhancing their confidence in the purchase.

Building Relationships With Buyers

Building strong relationships with buyers is key to creating a successful and sustainable cattle business. Start by establishing trust and credibility through transparent communication and high-quality service. Be responsive to inquiries, provide detailed information about your cattle, and address any concerns or questions promptly.

Consider offering value-added services, such as delivery options or ongoing support, to enhance your relationship with buyers. Providing excellent customer service and maintaining a professional attitude can lead to repeat business and positive word-of-mouth referrals. Build a network of satisfied customers who can vouch for the quality of your cattle and your reliability as a seller.

Networking within the industry is also important. Attend industry events, join agricultural associations, and engage with online communities to connect with potential buyers and industry professionals. By actively participating in these networks, you can stay informed about market trends and opportunities while strengthening your relationships with buyers.

CHAPTER NINE

Record Keeping And Management

Importance Of Accurate Records

Accurate record-keeping is crucial for successful cattle ranching. It ensures that you have detailed information about every aspect of your operation, which helps in making informed decisions and improving productivity. Keeping precise records allows you to track the health, breeding, and performance of your cattle, which is essential for identifying trends and addressing issues promptly. Without accurate records, you risk losing valuable data, which can lead to inefficiencies and increased costs.

Maintaining accurate records also helps in compliance with regulations and standards. Many regions require ranchers to keep detailed records of health and breeding practices to ensure the welfare of the animals. Moreover, having a clear record of your cattle's history aids in managing inventory, planning breeding programs, and optimizing the overall management of the herd.

Lastly, well-maintained records support better financial management. By keeping track of expenses, income, and investments, you can better manage your budget and assess the profitability of your ranch. This information is vital for making strategic decisions about scaling operations, investing in new equipment, or improving facilities.

Types Of Records To Maintain

In cattle ranching, several types of records are essential to maintain. Health records are crucial for monitoring the well-being of your cattle.

These records should include vaccination histories, treatments for diseases, and any other health-related events. By keeping detailed health records, you can ensure timely interventions and track the effectiveness of your health management practices.

Breeding records are another important type of record. These should document mating dates, breeding outcomes, and the lineage of each animal. Accurate breeding records help in managing genetic diversity, planning future breedings, and improving the overall quality of your herd. Tracking the performance of different sires and dams can guide your breeding decisions and enhance herd productivity.

Sales records are also necessary for managing the financial aspects of your ranch. These records should detail the sale of cattle, including sale dates, prices, and buyer information. Keeping accurate sales records helps in analyzing market trends, evaluating the profitability of your sales, and planning future marketing strategies.

Using Technology For Record-Keeping

Technology can greatly enhance record-keeping in cattle ranching. There are various software solutions and apps designed specifically for livestock management. These tools can automate record-keeping tasks, making it easier to track health, breeding, and sales data. For example, herd management software allows you to input and access data from any device, reducing the chances of errors and ensuring that information is always up-to-date.

Implementing RFID (Radio Frequency Identification) tags is another technological advancement that can streamline record keeping. RFID tags are attached to the cattle and can be scanned to quickly retrieve and update information about each animal.

This technology helps in tracking individual cattle, monitoring their movements, and recording health and breeding data in real time.

Additionally, cloud-based storage solutions provide a secure and accessible way to store and manage your records. By using cloud services, you can ensure that your data is backed up and can be accessed from anywhere, which is especially useful if you need to collaborate with other team members or access records while away from the ranch.

Financial Management And Budgeting

Effective financial management and budgeting are key components of running a successful cattle ranch. Start by creating a detailed budget that includes all potential expenses, such as feed, veterinary care, labor, and equipment.

This budget will serve as a financial roadmap and help you allocate resources efficiently.

Tracking income and expenses regularly is essential for staying within budget and assessing the financial health of your operation. Use accounting software or spreadsheets to record every transaction, categorize expenses, and monitor cash flow. Regularly reviewing your financial records helps in identifying areas where you can cut costs or invest more wisely.

Budgeting also involves planning for future investments. Evaluate your current resources and future needs to determine where additional funds may be required. This might include purchasing new equipment, expanding facilities, or investing in technology. By forecasting and planning for these expenses, you can ensure that your ranch remains financially stable and capable of growth.

Analyzing Data For Improved Decision-Making

Data analysis is a powerful tool for improving decision-making in cattle ranching. Start by collecting data from various sources, such as health records, breeding records, and financial statements. Once you have a comprehensive dataset, use analytical tools to identify trends, patterns, and correlations.

For example, analyzing health data can reveal common issues affecting your herd, allowing you to implement targeted health management strategies. Similarly, breeding data analysis can help in evaluating the performance of different sires and dams, guiding your breeding decisions to enhance herd quality.

Financial data analysis is also crucial for making informed decisions about investments and operational changes. By examining your financial records, you can assess the profitability of different aspects of your ranch, such as feed costs versus weight gain, and make adjustments to improve overall efficiency. Data-driven decision-making ensures that your actions are based on evidence rather than intuition, leading to more effective and strategic management of your cattle ranch.

CHAPTER TEN

Sustainable Ranching Practices

Benefits Of Sustainable Ranching

Sustainable ranching is an approach that seeks to balance the needs of livestock production with the preservation of natural resources and ecosystems. One major benefit is the enhancement of soil health. Through practices such as rotational grazing, the land is allowed to rest and recover, which improves soil fertility and structure. This not only boosts the growth of nutritious forage but also reduces soil erosion. Healthy soil contributes to better water retention and minimizes runoff, which is beneficial for both the environment and the rancher.

Another significant advantage of sustainable ranching is the improvement of animal welfare.

By focusing on the well-being of the livestock, sustainable practices often lead to healthier animals that require fewer medical interventions. For example, providing access to varied pastures and natural shelter can reduce stress and promote better overall health in cattle. This can translate into higher productivity and reduced costs for the rancher, as healthier animals are more efficient in converting feed into meat or milk.

Sustainable ranching also fosters economic resilience. By adopting diverse income streams, such as agrotourism or value-added products, ranchers can buffer against market fluctuations and environmental challenges. This approach encourages ranchers to engage in practices that not only sustain but also enhance the long-term productivity of their land, ensuring that their operation remains viable and profitable in the face of changing conditions.

Soil And Water Conservation Techniques

Effective soil and water conservation are crucial components of sustainable ranching. One fundamental technique is rotational grazing, where livestock are moved between different pastures or paddocks to prevent overgrazing in any one area. This method allows vegetation to recover and helps maintain soil structure. Implementing a well-planned grazing system also reduces soil compaction and promotes the growth of deep-rooted plants, which enhances soil health and water infiltration.

Another important practice is the use of cover crops and forage legumes. Planting cover crops during the off-season or alongside primary forage crops helps to protect the soil from erosion and improve its organic matter content. Legumes, in particular, fix nitrogen in the soil, which reduces the need for synthetic fertilizers and enhances the nutrient profile of the pasture. This not only supports soil fertility but also improves the quality of the forage available to livestock.

Water conservation can be achieved through the installation of water catchment systems and efficient irrigation practices. Collecting rainwater in cisterns or ponds for later use reduces dependency on groundwater sources and helps manage water resources more effectively. Additionally, employing techniques such as drip irrigation or using soil moisture sensors ensures that water is applied where and when it is needed, minimizing waste and optimizing crop growth.

Integrating Wildlife And Biodiversity

Integrating wildlife and biodiversity into ranching practices promotes ecological balance and enhances the resilience of the ranching system. One effective strategy is to maintain natural habitats within and around grazing areas. Creating buffer zones with native vegetation or leaving certain areas untouched provides habitats for local wildlife and supports a range of species. This not only benefits the ecosystem but also helps control pests and diseases, which can reduce the need for chemical interventions.

Incorporating diverse plant species in pastures and forage areas can enhance biodiversity. Diverse plantings attract a variety of beneficial insects and microorganisms, which contribute to a healthier ecosystem. For example, planting flowering plants can attract pollinators, while different grass species can support various soil organisms. This diversity improves soil health and forage quality, creating a more sustainable environment for both livestock and wildlife.

Ranchers can also engage in conservation programs and partnerships with environmental organizations. These collaborations often provide financial incentives and technical support for implementing biodiversity-friendly practices. For instance, participating in habitat restoration projects or wildlife management plans can contribute to broader conservation goals while aligning with sustainable ranching objectives.

Reducing Carbon Footprint

Reducing the carbon footprint of ranching involves several strategies aimed at minimizing greenhouse gas emissions and enhancing carbon sequestration. One approach is to improve the efficiency of feed use. By selecting feed with a higher nutritional value and optimizing feeding practices, ranchers can reduce methane emissions from enteric fermentation in livestock.

Additionally, supplementing cattle diets with additives such as seaweed or specific grains has been shown to lower methane production.

Implementing energy-efficient technologies and practices on the ranch can also reduce carbon emissions. This includes using renewable energy sources like solar or wind power for electricity, as well as optimizing the use of diesel and fuel in machinery. Energy-efficient buildings and infrastructure, such as well-insulated barns and efficient irrigation systems, further contribute to reducing the overall carbon footprint of the operation.

Carbon sequestration can be enhanced through practices like agroforestry and reforestation. Planting trees and maintaining wooded areas within or around grazing lands helps capture carbon dioxide from the atmosphere and store it in biomass and soil. This not only mitigates greenhouse gas emissions but also provides additional benefits such as improved soil health and habitat for wildlife.

Future Trends In Sustainable Ranching

The future of sustainable ranching is shaped by ongoing advancements in technology and growing awareness of environmental issues. Precision agriculture technologies, such as GPS-guided equipment and remote sensing, are expected to become more prevalent. These tools enable ranchers to monitor and manage their resources with greater accuracy, leading to more efficient use of inputs and reduced environmental impact.

Another emerging trend is the integration of data analytics and artificial intelligence into ranch management. By analyzing data on soil health, weather patterns, and livestock performance, ranchers can make more informed decisions and optimize their practices. This data-driven approach allows for precise adjustments to grazing systems, feed management, and conservation efforts, enhancing the sustainability of the operation.

Consumer demand for sustainably produced food is also likely to drive changes in ranching practices. As consumers become more environmentally conscious, they increasingly seek out products that are certified as sustainable or organic. This trend encourages ranchers to adopt practices that align with these values and to communicate their sustainability efforts effectively. By embracing these trends, ranchers can not only contribute to environmental stewardship but also enhance their market position and profitability.

CHAPTER ELEVEN

Dealing With Challenges And Risks

Identifying Common Challenges In Cattle Ranching

Cattle ranching, while a rewarding venture, presents a variety of challenges that can affect both novice and experienced ranchers. One of the primary challenges is managing herd health. Cattle are susceptible to a range of diseases and parasites, which can impact their growth, reproduction, and overall productivity. Preventive measures, such as vaccinations and regular health check-ups, are crucial. Establishing a relationship with a veterinarian who specializes in cattle can help in diagnosing and treating diseases early.

Another significant challenge is ensuring proper nutrition for the herd. Cattle require a balanced diet to maintain their health and productivity. Providing adequate feed and supplements, especially during periods of low forage availability, is essential. Understanding the nutritional needs of different cattle breeds and stages of production helps in formulating an appropriate feeding plan. Additionally, the cost of high-quality feed and supplements can be substantial, necessitating careful financial planning and budgeting.

Water availability is also a critical concern. Cattle need a constant supply of clean, fresh water to thrive. Inadequate water supply can lead to reduced feed intake and poor overall health. Setting up reliable water sources and ensuring they are well-maintained is key. During drought conditions or in arid regions, implementing water conservation practices and exploring alternative water sources can mitigate this issue.

Risk Management Strategies

Effective risk management is essential for the success and sustainability of a cattle ranch. One fundamental strategy is to diversify your operations. Relying solely on cattle sales can be risky if market prices drop or if there are unexpected expenses. Diversification can include integrating crop production, agro-tourism, or other livestock types into your ranching operation. This not only spreads financial risk but also provides additional revenue streams.

Another critical aspect of risk management is financial planning. Maintaining a detailed budget and regularly monitoring cash flow helps in anticipating and managing financial challenges. Setting aside an emergency fund can provide a cushion for unexpected expenses, such as veterinary bills or equipment repairs. Additionally, obtaining insurance coverage for your livestock, property, and equipment can offer protection against unforeseen losses.

Implementing biosecurity measures is also crucial in managing risks. This includes practices such as controlling access to your ranch, sanitizing equipment and facilities, and monitoring the health of incoming cattle. These measures help prevent the introduction and spread of diseases that could have severe financial implications.

Coping With Market Fluctuations

Market fluctuations can significantly impact the profitability of cattle ranching. Prices for cattle can vary based on factors such as supply and demand, feed costs, and global market trends. To cope with these fluctuations, it's important to stay informed about market conditions and trends.

Regularly reviewing market reports and industry news can help you make informed decisions about when to buy or sell cattle.

Contract marketing is a strategy that can provide more stability in pricing. By negotiating contracts with buyers in advance, you can lock in prices and reduce the impact of market volatility. While this approach might limit the potential for higher profits if prices increase, it also provides certainty and helps in budgeting and planning.

Additionally, exploring value-added opportunities can help mitigate the effects of market fluctuations. This could involve processing cattle into meat products, participating in niche markets, or developing branded products. By adding value to your cattle, you can potentially command higher prices and reduce your dependence on fluctuating market prices.

Managing Environmental Risks (Drought, Floods)

Environmental risks, such as droughts and floods, pose significant challenges to cattle ranching. Droughts can lead to reduced forage availability and water shortages, while floods can damage pastures, and infrastructure, and contaminate water sources. Preparing for these risks involves proactive planning and implementation of mitigation strategies.

During drought conditions, managing forage and water resources becomes critical. This may involve rotating pastures to prevent overgrazing, supplementing feed and water, and implementing water conservation practices. Investing in infrastructure, such as water storage systems and drought-resistant forage crops, can help ensure adequate resources during dry periods.

Flood management involves protecting infrastructure and maintaining good drainage systems to prevent waterlogging. Elevating critical infrastructure, such as feed storage and animal shelters, can reduce the risk of damage. Additionally, having an emergency response plan in place, including evacuation procedures and flood insurance, can help you respond effectively to flooding events.

Building Resilience In Your Ranching Operation

Building resilience in your ranching operation involves developing strategies to adapt and thrive despite challenges. One approach is to invest in improving the health and productivity of your herd through selective breeding and proper animal husbandry practices.

Healthier cattle are more resilient to diseases and environmental stresses, enhancing the overall stability of your operation.

Adopting sustainable practices, such as rotational grazing and soil conservation, can improve land health and increase its capacity to withstand environmental stresses. These practices help maintain forage quality and soil fertility, which contribute to the long-term success of your ranching operation.

Networking with other ranchers and industry professionals can also enhance your resilience. Joining local ranching associations or participating in industry events provides opportunities to share knowledge, gain insights, and access resources. Building a strong support network can offer valuable advice and assistance in navigating challenges and seizing opportunities.

Frequently Ask Questions And Answer.

· **What is cattle ranching?**

Answer: Cattle ranching involves the breeding and raising of cattle for meat (beef), milk, or both. It includes managing the herd, grazing land, and maintaining facilities.

· **What are the primary breeds of cattle used in ranching?**

Answer: Common breeds include Angus, Hereford, Charolais, Simmental, and Holstein. Each breed has unique traits suited for different climates and purposes.

· How do ranchers manage cattle health?

Answer: Cattle health is managed through regular veterinary care, vaccinations, parasite control, proper nutrition, and monitoring for signs of illness.

· What kind of feed do cattle require?

Answer: Cattle typically require a balanced diet that includes forage (like grass or hay), grains, minerals, and water. The diet may vary depending on whether the cattle are grazing or being fed in a feedlot.

· What is the difference between free-range and feedlot cattle ranching?

Answer: Free-range cattle graze on pastures and have more space, while feedlot cattle are confined and fed a controlled diet to promote faster growth.

· **How do ranchers manage grazing to prevent overgrazing?**

Answer: Ranchers use rotational grazing techniques, which involve moving cattle between different pastures to allow grass to recover and prevent overgrazing.

· **What are the environmental impacts of cattle ranching?**

Answer: Environmental impacts include land degradation, deforestation, greenhouse gas emissions, and water use. Sustainable practices aim to minimize these effects.

· **How can ranchers improve cattle genetics?**

Answer: By selecting and breeding cattle with desirable traits such as better growth rates, disease resistance, and higher quality meat, ranchers can improve herd genetics.

· **What are the benefits of using technology in cattle ranching?**

Answer: Technology can enhance efficiency through tools like electronic tagging for tracking, automated feeders, and data management systems for monitoring herd health and production.

· **What is the role of cattle ranching in the economy?**

Answer: Cattle ranching contributes to the economy by providing beef and dairy products, creating jobs, and supporting related industries like feed production and veterinary services.

· **How do ranchers ensure cattle welfare?**

Answer: Ensuring cattle welfare involves providing adequate shelter, food, water, medical care, and handling practices that minimize stress and injury.

· **What are common challenges faced in cattle ranching?**

Answer: Challenges include managing feed costs, dealing with diseases and pests, maintaining land and equipment, and adapting to changing market conditions and regulations.

· **How do ranchers manage water resources for cattle?**

Answer: Ranchers manage water resources by providing access to clean water sources, using water conservation practices, and ensuring proper maintenance of water infrastructure.

· **What is the process of cattle breeding?**

Answer: Cattle breeding involves selecting animals with desirable traits and mating them to produce offspring. This can be done through natural mating or artificial insemination.

· **How do weather conditions affect cattle ranching?**

Answer: Extreme weather conditions such as droughts, floods, or cold temperatures can impact cattle health, feed availability, and overall productivity.

· **What are some best practices for handling cattle?**

Answer: Best practices include using low-stress handling techniques, ensuring proper facilities and training staff to work safely and effectively with cattle.

· **How is beef quality graded?**

Answer: Beef quality is graded based on factors like marbling, tenderness, color, and age of the animal. Common grading systems include USDA Prime, Choice, and Select.

- **What are the regulations affecting cattle ranching?**

Answer: Regulations can vary by region but typically include standards for animal welfare, environmental protection, food safety, and land use.

- **How does cattle ranching impact local communities?**

Answer: Cattle ranching can support local communities through job creation, economic activity, and preserving open spaces. However, it can also pose challenges like resource competition.

- **What are the trends in modern cattle ranching?**

Answer: Modern trends include increased use of technology, sustainable practices, focus on animal welfare and direct-to-consumer marketing.

CONCLUSION

Cattle ranching, a cornerstone of global agriculture and economy, is undergoing profound transformations as it navigates the complexities of modern challenges and opportunities. This conclusion aims to encapsulate the essence of cattle ranching's evolution, its current state, and its prospects.

Historically, cattle ranching has been integral to the development of societies, contributing to economic stability, food security, and cultural heritage. It has provided livelihoods for millions and has shaped landscapes across continents. From its early days, when cattle were primarily raised for meat, milk, and leather, to the present, where it encompasses a wide range of activities including beef production, dairy farming, and conservation efforts, the industry has demonstrated remarkable adaptability and resilience.

In contemporary times, cattle ranching faces several critical challenges. Environmental concerns have become increasingly prominent, with the industry being scrutinized for its contributions to deforestation, greenhouse gas emissions, and biodiversity loss. Sustainable practices are now at the forefront of discussions, urging ranchers to adopt strategies that balance productivity with environmental stewardship. Advances in technology and science, such as precision farming, genetic improvements, and alternative feed solutions, offer promising avenues to enhance sustainability and reduce the ecological footprint of cattle ranching.

Economic pressures are also significant. Market fluctuations, global trade dynamics, and rising operational costs can impact profitability. Ranchers must navigate these uncertainties while striving to maintain high standards of animal welfare and product quality.

Diversification and value-added products are becoming essential strategies for mitigating risks and maximizing returns.

On a positive note, there is a growing movement towards regenerative agriculture, which seeks to restore soil health, enhance biodiversity, and sequester carbon. Many cattle ranchers are embracing these principles, seeing them not only as a way to contribute to environmental conservation but also as a means to improve the resilience and productivity of their operations.

Looking ahead, the future of cattle ranching will likely be shaped by continued innovation and collaboration. Stakeholders from all sectors—ranchers, scientists, policymakers, and consumers—must work together to address the pressing issues and seize opportunities for improvement. Embracing sustainable practices, leveraging technology, and fostering a greater understanding of the role of cattle ranching in global food systems will be key to ensuring its long-term viability and positive impact.

In conclusion, while cattle ranching faces significant challenges, it also holds immense potential for positive change. By embracing sustainability and innovation, the industry can continue to play a vital role in global agriculture, supporting both economic prosperity and environmental stewardship.

THE END